P9-CCE-228

WITHDRAWN

J
R
T

Kid Pick!

Title: _____

Author: _____

Picked by: _____

_____

Why I love this book:

_____
_____
_____

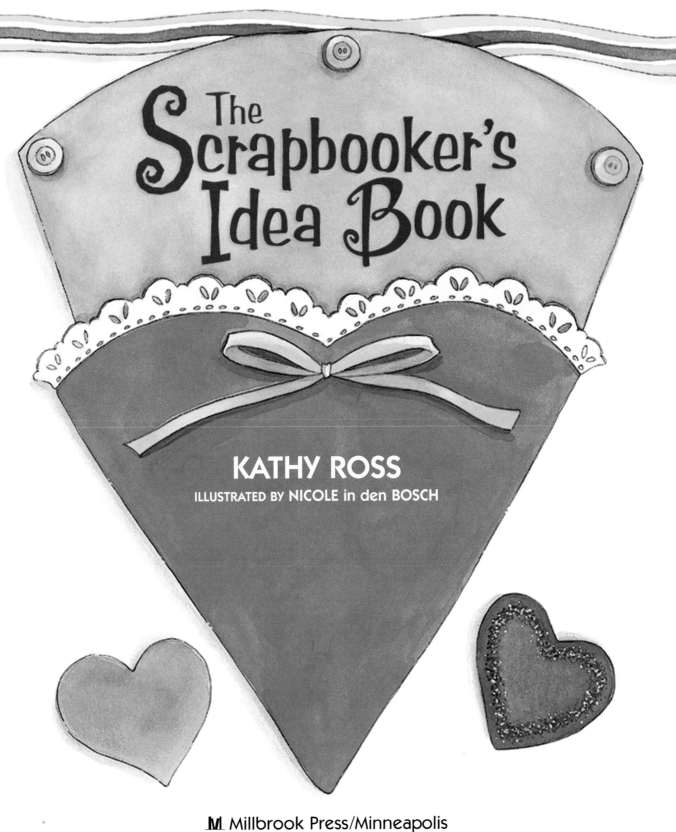

The Scrapbooker's Idea Book

KATHY ROSS

ILLUSTRATED BY NICOLE in den BOSCH

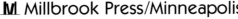

M Millbrook Press/Minneapolis

To my sister, Lee, who makes the best scrapbooks ever!

Millbrook Press, Inc.
A division of Lerner Publishing Group
241 First Avenue North
Minneapolis, Minnesota 55401 U.S.A.

Web site address: www.lernerbooks.com

Library of Congress Cataloging-in-Publication Data

Ross, Kathy (Katharine Reynolds), 1948–
        The scrapbooker's idea book / by Kathy Ross ; illustrated by Nicole in den Bosch.
        p. cm. — (Girl crafts)
Includes bibliographical references.
    ISBN-13: 978-0-7613-2777-6 (lib. bdg. : alk. paper)
    ISBN-10: 0-7613-2777-0 (lib. bdg. : alk. paper)
        1. Paper work. 2. Scrapbooks. I. Bosch, Nicole in den. II. Title.
        III. Series: Ross, Kathy (Katharine Reynolds), 1948- Girl crafts.
    TT870.R57825 2007
    745.593--dc22   2005024533

Manufactured in the United States of America
1 2 3 4 5 6 – JR – 12 11 10 09 08 07

Contents

It is helpful to have a place to store the things you want to include in your scrapbook as you collect them.

Cereal Box File

Here is what you need:

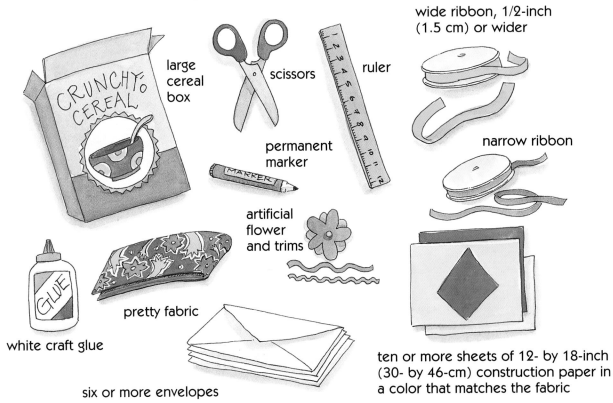

large cereal box

scissors

ruler

wide ribbon, 1/2-inch (1.5 cm) or wider

permanent marker

narrow ribbon

artificial flower and trims

white craft glue

pretty fabric

six or more envelopes

ten or more sheets of 12- by 18-inch (30- by 46-cm) construction paper in a color that matches the fabric

Here is what you do:

1. Cut the top, bottom, and one side from the cereal box so that you are left with a cardboard file, with the remaining side of the box now becoming the back of the file.

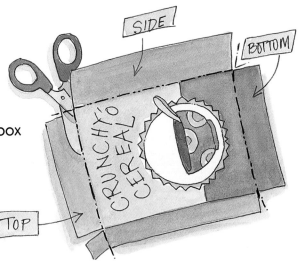

4

2. Cut a piece of fabric about 2 inches (5 cm) larger all around than the outside of the box file.

3. Cover the outside of the box with glue. Then apply the fabric carefully, folding the edges of the fabric over the edges of the box as if you were wrapping a package. Glue the edges to the inside of the box to secure.

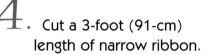

4. Cut a 3-foot (91-cm) length of narrow ribbon.

5. Cover the inside of the box with glue.

6. Lay the ribbon across the center of the box so that the two ends come out of the box on each side at the top of the file to form ties to close the file.

7. Glue a sheet of construction paper over the inside of the box to cover the center part of the ribbon and the edges of the fabric. Trim away any excess paper from the edges.

8. Cut a 6-inch (15-cm) piece of the wide ribbon for each file category you are going to make. The categories you choose will depend on the type of things you are saving to put in your scrapbook. See page 6 for my list.

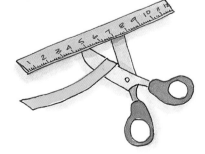

(continued on next page)

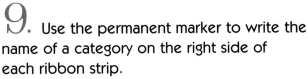

9. Use the permanent marker to write the name of a category on the right side of each ribbon strip.

10. Fold six or more sheets of construction paper in half to make files. Trim the files to fit inside the box file.

11. Glue an envelope to the back inside of each file to hold small items.

12. Glue the front of the first file to the front of the inside of the box file.

13. Glue the front of the second file to the back of the first file. The left end of a ribbon strip category should be in between so that the name of the file sticks out on the right side of the file.

14. Continue to glue all the files together, putting each ribbon strip just below the one before it so that they do not cover up one another.

15. Glue the last file to the back of the file box.

16. Decorate the outside of the file with the trims and the artificial flower.

This is a great way to keep track of all the special bits and pieces you are saving to put into your scrapbook. I made categories for memorabilia (photos, tickets, and notes), scenes (big magazine pages with full-color scenes that make nice pages for a scrapbook), and paper dolls (collected from magazines and printed online). You might want other categories such as craft ideas, recipes, Web pages to visit, things to send away for, or greeting cards you want to save.

Three-dimensional mementos can be saved using discarded plastic blister packs.

Blister-Pack Savers

Here is what you need:

flat types of plastic blister packs such as those used for stationery labels

scissors

markers

white craft glue

trims

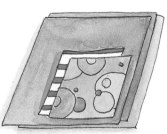

construction paper or patterned paper

Here is what you do:

1. Cut a piece of paper to line the inside back of the plastic blister pack. If you wish, you can use the markers to write any information about the item you are saving either on the page of the scrapbook or on the cut paper backing of the blister pack.

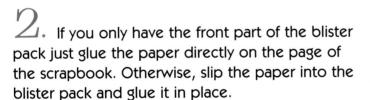

2. If you only have the front part of the blister pack just glue the paper directly on the page of the scrapbook. Otherwise, slip the paper into the blister pack and glue it in place.

3. Place the item on the paper-covered page or inside the blister pack and glue the edges of the blister back over the paper backing and the item.

4. If the blister pack has a back, you will need to glue it into the book now.

5. Decorate the edges of the pack with trim of your choice.

Seashells from the Beach

This is a great way to keep tiny treasures safe while still being able to see them.

Pretty gift bags can become pretty scrapbooks!

Gift Bag Scrapbook

Here is what you need:

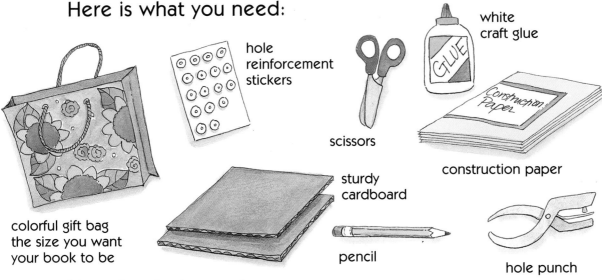

hole reinforcement stickers

white craft glue

scissors

construction paper

colorful gift bag the size you want your book to be

sturdy cardboard

pencil

hole punch

Here is what you do:

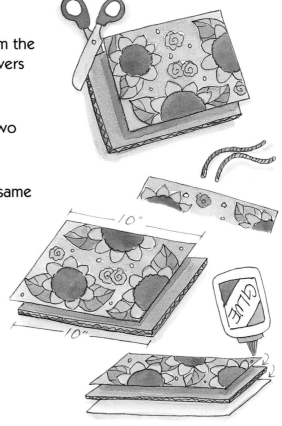

1. Cut the front and back panels from the gift bag to use as the front and back covers of the scrapbook.

2. Untie the two handles from the two sides of the gift bag and remove them.

3. Cut two pieces of cardboard the same size as the front and back covers of the scrapbook.

4. Glue a piece of cardboard to the back of each cover to make it more sturdy.

5. For a more finished look, cut a piece of construction paper and glue it over the inside of each cover.

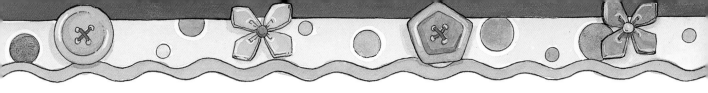

6. Cut construction paper pages for the book the same size as the covers.

7. Line the pages up with the two holes that were left when you removed the handle from the front cover panel.

8. Use the pencil to mark the pages through the two holes in the cover.

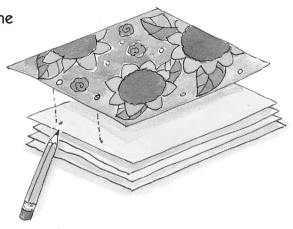

9. Use the hole punch to punch holes in the pages.

10. Cover each hole with a reinforcement sticker to help prevent the page from tearing out of the book with use.

11. Line the holes in the pages up with the front and back covers of the book. Use the two handles removed from the bag to tie the book together through the holes. Do not tie the book too tight or it will be difficult to turn the pages.

You can easily add more pages to this book later by removing the two ties.

Attractive catalogs make great scrapbooks.

Catalog Scrapbook

Here is what you need:

old catalog with
lots of attractive,
colorful pictures

craft paints
and a paintbrush

rickrack and
other trims

white
craft glue

scissors

variety of pretty
wrapping paper

Here is what you do:

1. Use the craft paint to paint over any writing on the pages of the catalog so that only the pictures are left exposed. It is best to do this two open pages at a time so that the paint can dry without sticking to the opposite page. Use different colors on the different pages.

2. For variety, cover some of the pages in the catalog by gluing pretty wrapping paper over them.

3. You can use either or both of the techniques in Step 1 and Step 2 to do the cover of the scrapbook.

4. This scrapbook lends itself well to making "envelope" pages. These are wonderful for storing items like paper dolls in the book. To make an envelope page, fold the right-hand page in toward the center of the book. The size of the envelope will depend on where you decide to fold the page.

5. Glue the sides of the folded paper to the edges of the page on the left to create an envelope.

6. Fold the end of the unfolded page down over the envelope to create a flap.

7. You might want to decorate the flap by gluing on strips of rickrack or other trim.

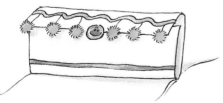

You could make an entire scrapbook of envelope pages to store your paper dolls or memorabilia. Remember that you will not need to paint the pages that form the inside of the envelopes.

Paper plates make the perfect scrapbook for recipes clipped from magazines and fliers.

Paper Plate Recipe Scrapbook

Here is what you need:

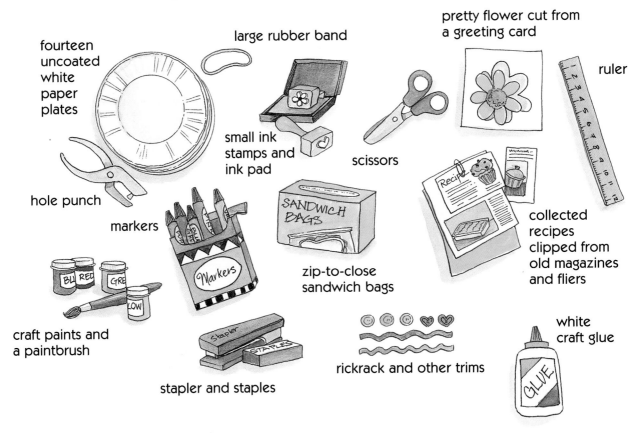

fourteen uncoated white paper plates

large rubber band

pretty flower cut from a greeting card

ruler

small ink stamps and ink pad

scissors

hole punch

markers

collected recipes clipped from old magazines and fliers

craft paints and a paintbrush

zip-to-close sandwich bags

white craft glue

rickrack and other trims

stapler and staples

Here is what you do:

1. Punch two holes, about 3 inches (8 cm) apart, through the rim of one of the paper plates. Then use a marker to mark the location of the holes on the second plate before punching them out. Do this with all of the plates.

2. Decorate the edges of all the paper plates to look like china plates. Use different materials for each plate. You can give the plate a border using markers, paint, glued-on trims, or a design made from ink stamps. Make each plate your own creative work of art.

3. Cut the rubber band through one side so that it forms a rubber string.

4. Thread one end of the rubber string up through one set of the holes in the plates and down through the other set of holes.

5. Tie the ends of the rubber string together to make a book of paper plates.

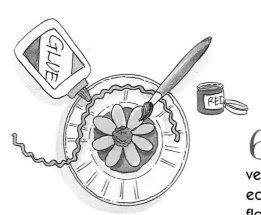

6. Decorate the front of the book like a very fancy china plate. Glue trim around the edges. Paint the center of the plate. Glue the flower cutout in the center.

7. Staple a zip-to-close sandwich bag to the center of each page if you are going to give the book to someone to use to hold clipped recipes. You can also glue your own clipped recipes to the center of each plate page.

Paper plate recipe scrapbooks make great gifts.

Making frames to slide your photos in is another way to
safely display them in your scrapbook.

Three Photo Frames

Here is what you need:

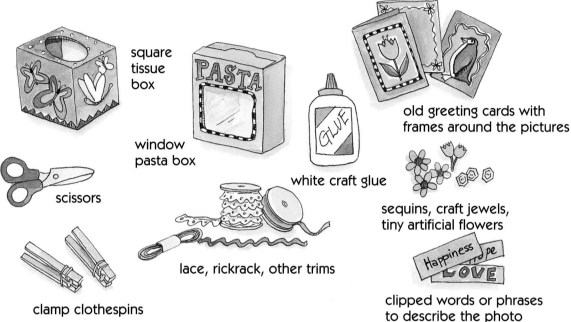

square
tissue
box

window
pasta box

white craft glue

old greeting cards with
frames around the pictures

scissors

lace, rickrack, other trims

sequins, craft jewels,
tiny artificial flowers

clamp clothespins

clipped words or phrases
to describe the photo

Here is what you do:

Tissue Box Frame

1. Cut the top and one side out of
the tissue box. Choose a smooth, complete side
rather than a side that has the two pieces of the
box coming together in the middle.

2. Fold the side of the box behind the top of
the box so that it becomes the back part of the
frame opening.

3. Glue two sides of the front and the back frames together, leaving an open side at either the top or the side to allow a photo to be inserted. Use clamp clothespins to hold the front and back together until the glue dries.

4. You might want to cut a small design out of the tissue box scraps to glue on one corner of the frame as a decoration. This does not work with all the designs, but boxes that are printed with pictures of birds, butterflies, or large flowers work well.

5. You might need to trim the photo to slip it into the frame.

6. Glue the back of the frame to a page in your scrapbook.

Pasta Box Frame

1. Cut around the cellophane window of a pasta box.

2. Cut an identical size piece from the pasta box scraps to use as a back for the frame.

3. Glue the two sides and the bottom of the frame front and back together.

(continued on next page)

4. Decorate the frame with sequins or tiny flowers if you wish.

5. Trim the photo to fit the frame, then slip it in.

6. Glue the back of the frame to a page in your scrapbook.

Greeting-Card Frame

1. Cut the picture out of the front of a framed greeting card so that only the back of the card and the edge are left.

2. Glue the back outer edges of the frame to the back of the card to make the frame.

3. Decorate the frame with sequins or trim. Find a word or phrase ("Happiness" or "You are wonderful!") clipped from an old card or magazine that goes well with the photo. Glue the word or phrase to the top of the card.

4. Trim the photo if needed to fit in the frame, then slip it in. Glue the back of the frame to a page in your scrapbook.

Try using all three of these photo frame ideas in your scrapbook!

Photos are a wonderful addition to any scrapbook.

Envelope Photo Corners

Here is what you need:

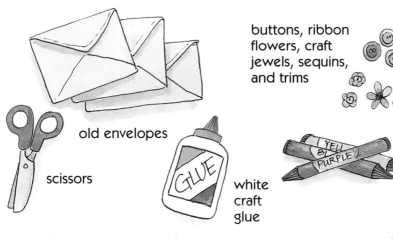

old envelopes

buttons, ribbon flowers, craft jewels, sequins, and trims

scissors

white craft glue

markers

Here is what you do:

1. Cut the four corners off one of the envelopes.

2. Color the fronts of the four corners if desired.

3. Decorate the four corners by gluing on one type of collage item from the suggested list above.

4. Slide a corner over each corner of the photo you wish to put in your book.

5. Put a dab of glue on the back of each corner and stick the corners to the page.

By using photo corners, you do not damage the photo with glue. Because the photos can easily be slipped out of the corners, you can change the photos on a page if you wish

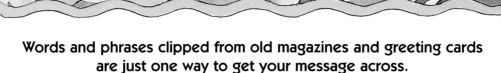

Words and phrases clipped from old magazines and greeting cards are just one way to get your message across.

Ideas for Fun and Fancy Words

Here is what you need:

pipe cleaners

large colored paper clips

cardboard

colored glue

yarn

scissors

water

white craft glue

clear plastic wrap

disposable container and craft stick for mixing

pencil

Here is what you do:

Make a pattern of the word you are going to use to be sure that the size and length are correct for the page. To do this, write the word on the cardboard and cover it with plastic wrap. The pattern is helpful for shaping the pipe-cleaner words. The yarn and colored glue words can actually be formed over the pattern.

Pipe-Cleaner Words

Use colorful pipe cleaners to shape words written in cursive. You can make the words all one color or switch to a different color when a second pipe cleaner is needed to finish.

Colored Glue Words

1. Use the colored glue to squeeze out a word right on the plastic wrap covering the pattern word.

2. When the glue has completely dried, peel the word off the plastic wrap and stick it in your book. Secure it with a few dabs of glue on the back.

Yarn Words

1. Use the craft stick to mix one part glue with one part water in the disposable container.

2. Cut a length of yarn long enough to write the entire word you are making.

3. Soak the yarn in the glue mixture to saturate it. Pull the yarn out one side of the tub, using the stick to squeeze out the excess glue mixture from the yarn.

4. Shape the yarn into a cursive word on the plastic wrap.

(continued on next page)

5. Let the yarn dry completely before peeling the word off the plastic wrap.

6. Use dabs of glue to stick the word to a page in your scrapbook.

Paper-Clip Letters

1. Shape each paper clip into a letter for the word you need. For letters like T and E you will need to break off a piece to shape the letter.

2. Paper clips can also be bent into simple shapes, such as a heart or an apple, to enhance your scrapbook page. Pieces of paper clip in more than one color can be used.

3. Attach the paper-clip letters and simple shapes to the scrapbook page with dabs of glue.

Using three-dimensional letters and words adds interest and fun to your scrapbook pages.

Store a collection of similar items in a scrapbook pocket.

Scrapbook Pockets

Here is what you need:

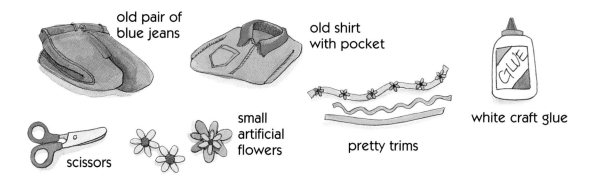

old pair of blue jeans

old shirt with pocket

white craft glue

scissors

small artificial flowers

pretty trims

Here is what you do:

1. Cut the back pocket from a pair of old jeans—or you could use the pocket from an old shirt.

2. Glue the pocket to a page in your scrapbook.

3. Decorate the pocket by gluing on trims and artificial flowers.

4. Cut some simple shapes, such as hearts, from the remaining jeans fabric. Glue the shapes around the pocket to decorate the page.

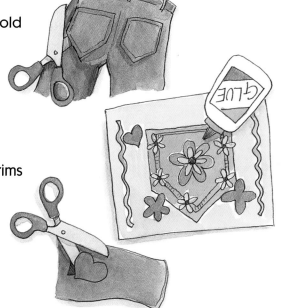

Scrapbook pockets are perfect for storing small collections of memorabilia. You could store plastic card "room keys" from hotels you have stayed in or movie tickets to keep a record of the movies you have seen. Pockets are also perfect for holding small notes, clipped pictures, and found items such as bird feathers and pretty pebbles. What's in your pocket?

Make holiday pockets for your scrapbook using old party hats.

Party Hat Pockets

Here is what you need:

red party hat

glitter

ruffle lace trim

sequins and craft jewels

green party hat

white craft glue

red construction paper

thin pink ribbon

markers

gold sparkle stems

scissors

rickrack or other trims

Here is what you do:

Heart Pocket

1. Flatten the red party hat with the seam at the center of the back of the hat.

2. Holding the flattened hat with the point at the bottom, make a heart shape by cutting two bumps through both layers of the hat's rim.

3. Glue the back of the heart to the scrapbook page.

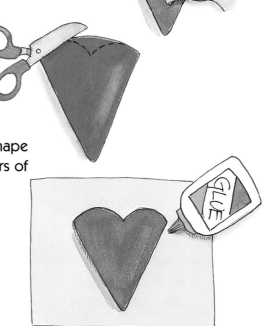

4. Decorate the top of the heart by gluing on ruffle lace.

5. Tie a piece of thin ribbon into a bow. Glue the bow to the front of the top of the heart.

6. Decorate the page around the heart pocket by gluing on trims.

7. Cut a heart from red construction paper.

8. Write "Valentines from My Friends" and the date.

9. Decorate the edges of the construction paper heart with glued-on glitter.

10. Glue the paper heart to the page.

Christmas Tree Pocket

1. Flatten the green hat with the seam at the center of the back of the hat.

2. Decorate the green party hat to look like a Christmas tree by gluing on pretty sequins and craft jewels.

(continued on next page)

3. You might also want to wrap some sparkle stems around the tree for garlands. Use dabs of glue to secure the stems.

4. Turn the tree upside down to form a pocket.

5. Glue the tree to the center of the scrapbook page.

6. Glue sequins on the page around the pocket to decorate it.

7. Use the pocket to save tiny Christmas items such as gift tags and tiny package tie-ons.

You might want to add a scrapbook clamp (page 48) to the page to display a favorite item from the pocket. These two page ideas allow you to tuck things into your scrapbook without using glue.

Make a scrapbook full of rooms and scenes for your magazine paper doll collection.

Paper Doll Rooms Scrapbook

Here is what you need:

old home and garden catalogs and magazines

white craft glue

light cardboard

magazine or online printed paper dolls

envelopes

tiny trims, flower sequins, and other collage materials

scissors

markers

Here is what you do:

1. Glue a paper doll to light cardboard to make the doll stiff. Cut the doll out.

2. Cut a 1-inch (2.5-cm) triangle from the cardboard.

3. Glue one side of the triangle to the bottom of the back of the paper doll so that the point sticks out from the bottom of the doll. This will be the tab used to slip the doll into the paper scenes in the scrapbook.

(continued on next page)

4. Choose full-page scenes from the old catalogs and magazines. Choose scenes that are in proportion to your doll. Most pages will need both sides of the open book covered, so look for two pages of scenes that work well together for each spread. For example, to make a bedroom one side could be a scene of a room and the other a bed.

5. A catalog scrapbook (page 10) is a good choice for this project.

6. Before you glue the scenes to the pages of the catalog scrapbook, you will need to cut a small slit in the scene anywhere you want a paper doll to stand. You might be able to find a scene with a picture of a bed that you can slit to slip the paper doll in for the night. This idea works well for the bathtub, too.

7. Glue the scenes to the pages of the catalog scrapbook by placing glue around the back edges of the page. Be careful not to glue the inner parts of the page or you might block the tab or paper doll when you try to slip it in the slit cut on the page.

8. Add tiny trims and fake flowers to the scenes to embellish them. For example, glue fake flowers over the picture of flowers in a vase or decorate a picture of a pillow with a bit of lace. Any collage material that is fairly flat can be added to the scenes.

9. Glue an envelope in the book for each paper doll you have "living" in the scrapbook rooms. Decorate the envelopes with trims and other collage materials. Use the envelopes to store the clothes for each paper doll. You might want to write the doll's name on the front of the envelope containing that doll's clothing.

Add additional rooms to the scrapbook over time to provide the dolls with all the different rooms and outdoor space they might need.

These pretty pages give you ways to display items that you don't want to permanently glue into your scrapbook.

Tuck-In Pages

Here is what you need:

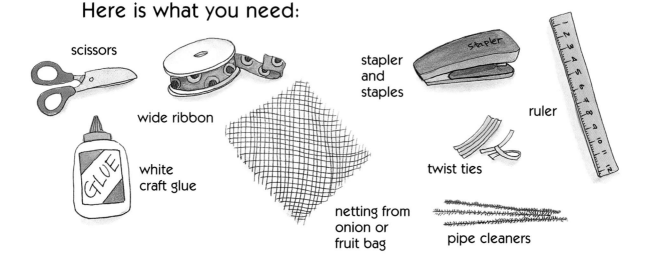

scissors

wide ribbon

white craft glue

netting from onion or fruit bag

stapler and staples

twist ties

pipe cleaners

ruler

Here is what you do:

Woven Ribbon Page

1. Fold a page in half toward the center of the scrapbook without creasing the center.

2. Cut slits from the fold to about 1 inch (2.5 cm) from the edge of the paper.

3. Open the page.

4. Cut pieces of ribbon to the height of the page.

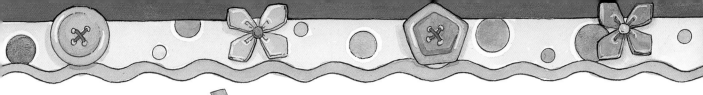

5. Weave the pieces of ribbon in and out through the slits in the page. Continue weaving ribbon across the page until the page is full of ribbon strips.

6. Trim the edges of the ribbon so that they are even with the ends of the page. Glue the ends of the ribbons in place to secure them.

7. Slip the corners of cards and photos between the woven ribbon and the page to hold them in the scrapbook.

Net-Covered Page

1. To make a different kind of tuck-in page, stretch the net bag over a page of the scrapbook.

2. Staple the net in place around the page.

3. Trim off the excess netting.

4. This page is perfect for tucking in things like bird feathers and flowers. Notes can also be tucked into the netting by the corners.

5. Simple words can be woven into the netting on the page using pieces of twist-ties or colorful pipe cleaners.

Try adding some tuck-in pages to your scrapbook.

A scrapbook journal is a book that uses photos, drawings and other clips, and memorabilia to illustrate the written entries.

Vintage-Look Scrapbook Journal

Here is what you need:

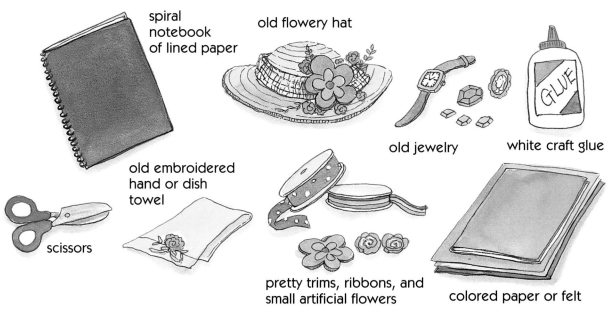

spiral notebook of lined paper

old flowery hat

old jewelry

white craft glue

GLUE

scissors

old embroidered hand or dish towel

pretty trims, ribbons, and small artificial flowers

colored paper or felt

Here is what you do:

1. To give your scrapbook journal a vintage look, you will need to look for an inexpensive flowery hat, embroidered hand or dish towel, or old broken jewelry at garage sales, flea markets, and rummage sales. Looking for pretty vintage items to craft with is lots of fun. If you are already going to sales with a grown-up, it will give you your own list of bargain finds to hunt for.

List to buy at Flea Market
1. Old Doll Clothes
2. Damaged Books
3. Vintage pattern fabric & wrapping paper
4. Old Buttons
5. Greeting Cards

2. Cover the outside of the notebook by wrapping a piece of felt or colored paper around the entire notebook and gluing it in place. Be sure to trim the felt or paper to fit with the notebook closed, not open, as additional fabric is needed to cover the spiral binder when the notebook is closed. Let the notebook dry in the closed position.

3. To use the trim from an old hat, carefully remove the flowers and the veil, too, if it has one, and glue all or part of the decorations to the cover of the covered scrapbook journal. Very fancy!

4. To use old jewelry, bend the clasps back and forth to remove them if the pieces need to be made flatter. Arrange the jewels in a pretty pattern on the front of the covered scrapbook journal and glue in place. Very glitzy!

5. To give a different vintage look, cover the scrapbook journal with a pretty dish or hand towel. Arrange the towel so that the embroidery is placed on the front of the book in a pleasing way. Wrap the towel around the outside of the notebook and glue it in place. Trim off the excess towel with the notebook closed. Let the glue dry with the notebook closed to ensure a good fit. Use complementing collage materials such as artificial flowers, ribbons, or trim to cover any holes or stains in the old towel. Very pretty!

You might come across some other garage sale "junk" that will be perfect for decorating the cover of your scrapbook journal.

When you look back at the pages of your scrapbook, it should tell about you and all the things you liked and did at that time.

Scrapbook Collage Pages About Me

Here is what you need:

box fronts and labels from your favorite foods

magazine pictures of your favorite TV shows

pictures and articles about favorite music CDs and performers

covers or title clips from favorite magazines and comic books

reviews and articles about movies you liked

pictures and small items to reflect your favorite sports and hobbies

covers of favorite books from catalogs, the Web, or hand drawn

favorite Web addresses and printouts from home pages

Here is what you do:

1. Collect items for any or all of the categories listed above. You might have some other ones to add. Store the items for each page in a separate zip-to-close bag until you are ready to do the page. If you made the cereal box file on page 4, this would also be a good place to store them.

2. Arrange the items on the page in a pleasing way. These pages offer the perfect opportunity to try some of the different page techniques in this book. If you are a big reader you might need a pocket to hold all the books you read this year. A page on favorite sports is the perfect place to use the magazine shape pictures and letters project found on page 36. Instead of making a food label collage page, you might want to arrange small grocery flier pictures of your favorite foods in a cupboard similar to the clothes closet idea found on page 40. The blister-pack holder on page 7 is perfect for holding collected seashells, and the woven page idea on page 28 is ideal for tucking in pressed flowers or feathers.

Make your pages a celebration of all the things that are a part of your life right now.

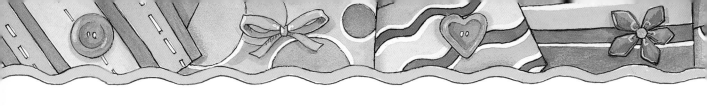

Box scrapbooks are a perfect way to display an entire scrapbook all at once.

Box Scrapbook

Here is what you need:

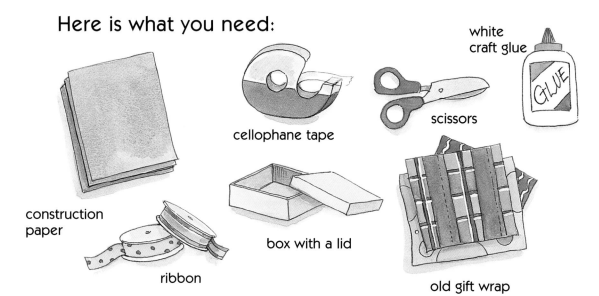

white craft glue

cellophane tape

scissors

construction paper

ribbon

box with a lid

old gift wrap

Here is what you do:

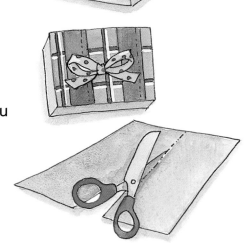

1. Cover the lid of the box by gluing on a piece of pretty gift wrap. If there is writing on the sides of the box that you wish to hide, cover the sides with paper, too.

2. Tie a piece of the ribbon in a bow and glue it onto the lid of the box.

3. Cut strips of construction paper as tall as the box and as long as the paper will allow. You will need enough strips to make at least ten sections in your scrapbook when the strips are attached and folded back and forth like a fan.

4. Use the cellophane tape to attach the strips of paper together to make one long strip.

5. Fold one end of the paper strip so that it exactly fits in the bottom of the box.

6. Continue folding the strip back and forth like a fan so that all the sections are the same size and fit in the box. Trim off any excess paper at the end.

7. Glue the back of one end of the strip in the bottom of the box.

8. Glue the back of the other end of the strip inside the lid. The folded paper should now fit neatly inside the box when the lid is on. To display the pages just stand the box and lid on end with the paper strip stretched out between them.

9. Larger box scrapbooks are perfect for saving bulky items such as a special seashell or pebble or a small party favor. You might want to add a couple of pockets (page 21 or 22) or staple in some zip-to-close bags to hold bulkier items.

The size of your book will depend on the size of the box you use. This idea works just as well with a small jewelry gift box as it does with a larger box such as a shoebox.

The colorful pages from old magazines are a great resource for your scrapbook.

Magazine Letters and Shapes

Here is what you need:

white craft glue

scissors

block letter stencils or patterns

old magazines with colorful pictures

simple shape stencils or patterns

pencil

Here is what you do:

TENNIS BALLS

1. Look through old magazines to find large, colorful pictures that are related to the theme of the page you are doing. For example, if it is a summertime page, find pictures of the outdoors with flowers, pools, the beach, beach balls—whatever reminds you of summer.

tennis

2. Use the block letter stencils or patterns to trace the letters of a word from the page. Position the letters on the picture so that something from the picture becomes part of the letter in a pleasing way. I found a page of striped summer T-shirts that I used to make my "striped T-shirt" letters. For a summer page you might want to cut out the word "sun" or "fun." Keep the words simple or you will end up with a page filled with the words and have no room to add anything else.

3. Another fun way to use the pictures is to cut simple shapes from them that are related to the overall picture. I found a page of flying birds and cut a bird shape from it, and I cut a flower shape from a page of flowers.

This project idea has endless possibilities and lots of room for your own creative interpretation.

Creating different backgrounds for your scrapbook pages is another way to add variety and interest to your book.

Scrapbook Background Pages

Here is what you need:

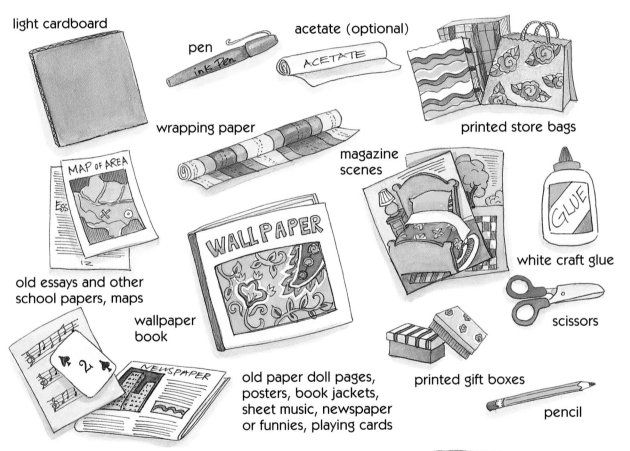

light cardboard

pen

ink Pen

acetate (optional)

ACETATE

wrapping paper

printed store bags

MAP OF AREA

Ess

magazine scenes

WALL PAPER

GLUE

white craft glue

old essays and other school papers, maps

wallpaper book

scissors

old paper doll pages, posters, book jackets, sheet music, newspaper or funnies, playing cards

NEWSPAPER

printed gift boxes

pencil

Here is what you do:

1. Collect a variety of different kinds of discarded papers from the list above to use as backgrounds for the pages of your scrapbook.

2. Trace around a page of your scrapbook on light cardboard. Cut the traced shape out of the cardboard to use as a pattern for cutting out page covers.

3. Cut the paper to the size of the scrapbook page. Glue the paper over the page to create a new background color.

4. Be creative in the way you cut the paper. Try tracing the page shape on acetate with the pen to make a clear pattern to use for cutting paper at odd angles. The clear pattern will allow you to see exactly what part of the picture you will be cutting out.

5. Choose a paper background that is related to the theme of your page. Old school papers are perfect for a back-to-school page, and a map is a great background for a page about a special trip.

What other sources of paper can you think of to add to the list?

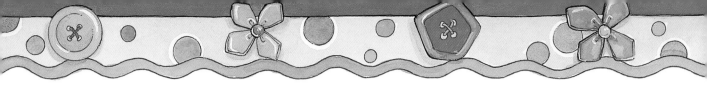

Make a page in your scrapbook that reflects your favorite clothing looks.

Scrapbook Clothes Closet

Here is what you need:

markers

small rubber band

white craft glue

construction paper

clothing catalogs, magazines, and fliers

small colored paper clips

pipe cleaner

scissors

two pony beads

trims

Here is what you do:

1. Use a sheet of construction paper that is the same size or smaller then the size of the scrapbook page. Fold the two sides of the paper in to meet at the center so that the two folds look like the two doors of a closet.

2. Glue the two ends of a piece of pipe cleaner inside the closet for a clothes bar.

3. Use the markers to add a shelf at the top of the closet for hats.

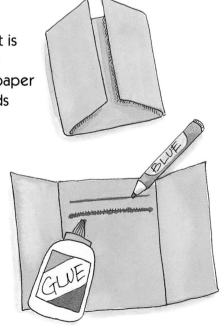

4. Shape the paper clips into hangers, using one of the curved ends of the paper clip to hang the hangers on the clothes bar.

5. Glue a pony bead to the edge of each closet door to look like the doorknob.

6. Use the trims and the markers to decorate the outside of the closet any way you wish.

7. Find clothes you like in the catalogs, magazines, and fliers. Choose clothing that is in proportion with the paper-clip hangers you have made.

8. Cut the clothing out. Don't forget to cut out some shoes and hats, too.

9. Glue each outfit to one side of a paper-clip hanger and hang it in the closet.

10. Glue the hats in the closet on the top shelf.

11. Glue the shoes in the bottom of the closet.

12. Put the rubber band across the two doorknobs to keep the closet shut.

Fill the closet with your favorite styles of clothing. It will be fun to look back at the closet in a few years to see what clothes were in style when you made your scrapbook.

An old and discarded book makes an interesting scrapbook.

Book Scrapbook

Here is what you need:

old book

white craft glue

trims, paper scraps

craft paints and a paintbrush

scissors

newspaper to work on

Here is what you do:

1. A great deal of the fun of this project is searching for the right old book to use. You might choose a book because of an interesting cover or because it has pretty pictures inside that you can incorporate into your scrapbook. Look for old books that might work for you at garage sales and used books sales at libraries.

2. If you choose a very thick book you may want to remove some of the pages to allow more room for your own scraps within the binding.

3. Paint the front and back covers of the book. Let the paint dry.

4. Decorate the front of the scrapbook with trims and cut paper pictures.

5. You can paint over the printed pages with a paint that covers or a watery paint that allows the print to show through. You can also just leave the printed pages as they are or glue background pages (page 38) over some or all of the pages being used.

6. If the book is one with illustrations, try to make the illustrations in the book a part of your scrapbook.

Scrapbooks made from old books will be as varied as the millions of old and discarded books out there waiting to be discovered and given a new use.

Old and broken jewelry can be used for scrapbook crafting.

Old Jewelry Scrapbook

Here is what you need:

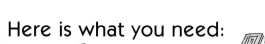 tiny hole punch

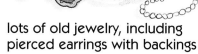 lots of old jewelry, including pierced earrings with backings

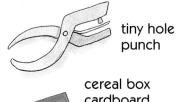 cereal box cardboard

 colored copier paper

 scissors

 white craft glue

 pencil

Here is what you do:

1. Cut a front and a back cover for the scrapbook from the cereal box cardboard that is the same size as the copier paper.

2. To cover the cardboard, glue a sheet of the copier paper to the front and the back of both covers.

3. Use the hole punch to punch two holes through the left side of the front and back covers near the top and the bottom.

4. Mark the color copier paper with pencil to show the location of the holes on what will be the left side of each of the ten to twelve inner pages of the book.

5. Fold the left side of the front cover to the left about an inch from the edge and rub a crease in the cardboard to make the book easier to open. This needs to be done while the glued paper is still wet to prevent any tearing.

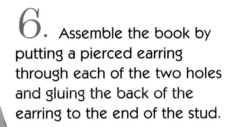

6. Assemble the book by putting a pierced earring through each of the two holes and gluing the back of the earring to the end of the stud.

7. Decorate the front of the book by gluing on pieces of old jewelry.

It is important that the glued earrings do not have too much stress on them or they will need to be re-glued. By using a limited number of pages of thin paper and folding the side of the front cover ahead of time, the earring fasteners should hold your book together with no trouble.

Clipped pictures are used to answer personal questions about yourself in this scrapbook.

Personal Preferences Scrapbook

Here is what you need:

pen

hole punch

white craft glue

old wallpaper (or other paper for pages)

lots of old catalogs, magazines, and greeting cards for pictures

markers

string

scissors

ruler

scrap paper

Here is what you do:

1. Use the pen and the scrap paper to make a list of twenty different categories about yourself, one for each page of the scrapbook. You can list very traditional categories like favorite foods, books, movies, and some more challenging categories such as what you dislike and your last thought at night. The idea is to make this book a very personal reflection of you.

1. Best Friends
2. Favorite Teachers
3. Favorite Movie Stars
4. Weather I like
5. Weather I don't like
6. Cartoons
7. Yukky Things
8. Clothes I want

2. Cut the wallpaper or other paper into twenty-two 9- by 6-inch (23- by 15-cm) pages.

3. Stack twenty-one of the pages with the print side down. Place the last sheet over the pages, print side up to form the cover for the book.

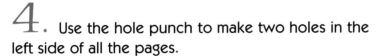

4. Use the hole punch to make two holes in the left side of all the pages.

5. Tie the pages together with a piece of the string to make the book.

6. Use the markers or the pen to write one category at the top of each page.

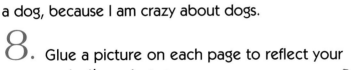

7. The challenge of this scrapbook is that you respond to each category with a picture rather than with words. Each page will have a picture clipped from a catalog, magazine, or other paper source to illustrate the category at the top. For example, on the page labeled "Favorite Activity" I glued a picture of a doll, because that is my hobby. On the page labeled "Something That Makes Me Smile" I put a picture of a dog, because I am crazy about dogs.

8. Glue a picture on each page to reflect your response to the category.

This little book should be a very personal reflection of who you are.

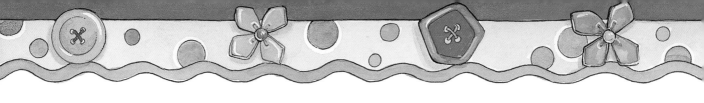

Add some pretty clamps to your book to hold items for future use or that you might want to change.

Scrapbook Clamp

Here is what you need:

clamp clothespin for each clamp you are making

1/2- inch (1.5-cm)- wide ribbon

craft paint and a paintbrush

BLUE RED YEL

white craft glue

scissors

sequins, buttons, craft jewels

trims

Here is what you do:

1. Cover one side of the clothespin by gluing on a strip of ribbon or painting it.

2. Decorate the covered or painted clothespin by gluing on trim, sequins, buttons, or craft jewels.

3. Glue a clamp in the front of your scrapbook to hold items for a page you are getting ready to work on.

Be Mine

Happy Holidays

Clamps are good for displaying something you have several of, such as greeting cards. Glue a large envelope in your scrapbook to hold the cards. Glue a clamp to the front of the envelope. This way you can change the card being featured on the page and enjoy all the cards you received without filling your book.